The Library of American Choreographers™

ALVIN AILEY

Judy Gitenstein

rosen
central™

The Rosen Publishing Group, Inc., New York

Published in 2006 by The Rosen Publishing Group, Inc.
29 East 21st Street, New York, NY 10010

First Edition

Library of Congress Cataloging-in-Publication Data

Gitenstein, Judy.
Alvin Ailey / Judy Gitenstein.
    p. cm. — (The library of American choreographers)
Includes bibliographical references and index.
ISBN 1-4042-0445-8 (lib. bdg.)
ISBN 1-4042-0639-6 (pbk. bdg.)
1. Ailey, Alvin—Juvenile literature. 2. Dancers—United States—
Biography—Juvenile literature. 3. Choreographers—United
States—Biography—Juvenile literature.
I. Title. II. Series.
GV1785.A38G58 2006
792.8'028'092—dc22

                                                                2005001946

Manufactured in the United States of America

On the cover: Alvin Ailey circa 1988. Background: Members of the
Alvin Ailey American Dance Theater performing "Wade in the Water"
from *Revelations*, 1977.

Contents

Introduction

"Dance is for everyone," Alvin Ailey often said. He wanted to make dance accessible to everyone. His goal was to create a dance company that gave African American dancers and choreographers a home to show their work. By the time of his death in 1989, that goal had not only been reached but surpassed. Nineteen million people have seen performances by the Alvin Ailey American Dance Theater since its first performance in 1958, more than any other modern dance company in the world.

Alvin Ailey's dances express to audiences what it feels like to be black in America in a way that speaks to all people, no matter what their age or race. His dances are about deep feelings, or "blood memories," as he called them. He portrayed his childhood church on a hot Sunday in Texas in his most famous piece, *Revelations*. He expressed

Alvin Ailey is pictured here in the 1950s. At the time Ailey entered the world of modern dance, many modern dance choreographers were searching for a way to reach a broader audience. Ailey would draw from folk sources and incorporate cultural themes to which a broader audience could relate.

how much he appreciated his mother in *Cry*. His dances were also based on political events. He took a strong stand against apartheid, or segregation, in South Africa in *Masekela Langage*.

Ailey poured his heart and soul into his choreography. His dances convey a deep emotion that speaks directly to a person's soul, in a language everyone understands no matter what language they speak.

Early Years in Texas

Alvin Ailey grew up during the Great Depression, a time of extreme poverty that gripped America from 1929 to 1939. It was also a time of racial segregation. To Alvin as a young boy, segregation meant that he and his friends were forced to sit upstairs when they went to the movies while the white children enjoyed better seats downstairs. It also meant that the elementary school that he and other African American students attended had old textbooks and almost no supplies, while the school for white students had new textbooks and better quality facilities.

Many Mouths to Feed

In 1931, the town of Rogers, Texas, in the Brazos River valley, had a population of just about 1,000 people. On January 5, 1931, the day that Alvin Ailey was born, thirteen of those people lived in one small house.

They were Alvin's paternal grandfather (his father's father), Alvin's parents, and his aunt and uncle and their eight children.

Alvin's arrival meant that there was one more mouth to feed. Alvin's father, Alvin Ailey Sr., wasn't able to find work to support his family, and when Alvin was just six months old, his father left the family. Alvin would see him only once more in his life, when he was about four. He would speak to him only once after that, on the phone, as a grown man.

Alvin's mother, Lula, was eighteen when Alvin was born. Lula was energetic and inventive, especially when it came to making a comfortable life for herself and her son. She didn't measure wealth in terms of money. To her, a rich life was about being strong and positive.

After Alvin Sr. left, Alvin and his mother moved to a cabin on a large farm. She did whatever she needed to do in order to find work. She picked cotton on the farm, did housekeeping, or washed and ironed clothing for white people. When Lula couldn't find a job, she and Alvin moved to another town so she could find work.

Insects and Chicken Snakes

Lula often took Alvin with her while she picked cotton

Alvin is pictured in this rare childhood photo at the age of fourteen with his stepfather, Fred Cooper. This photo was taken around the time of Ailey's first exposure to the world of dance.

in Wharton, Texas. He was independent and spent hours entertaining himself. He loved animals and nature. While living in Wharton, Alvin discovered a huge snake under the house. He would feed it every day with his own food. Very soon after his mother found out about this snake—and that he was feeding it food she worked so hard to put on the table—they moved, this time to Navasota, Texas, a town near Houston. Lula got a job at Memorial Hospital in Navasota. She was the first black woman to work there.

Many things in Navasota would influence Alvin's life. Their landlord in Navasota, Amos Alexander, became an important figure to Alvin. Alexander was a kind and generous man, and Alvin thought of him as the father he never got to know. Alexander gave Alvin a dog and let him ride the horses on the farm. He taught Alvin how to take care of the chickens and other small animals and how to plant and tend a garden. By this time, Alvin was nearly eight.

Alvin did well in elementary school. He was curious about the world around him. He carried a notebook and wrote stories and made sketches of insects and other things he saw. He loved to read and write, especially poetry. He also played the tuba. When Alvin was in fourth grade, the school principal realized that Alvin's mother didn't have enough money to pay for his tuba, so he bought the instrument for Alvin.

Alvin's mother spent long hours at work, and Alvin spent long hours alone or staying with relatives. He would turn to his

About Spirituals

The words in spirituals have many layers of meaning. Spirituals, first sung in the nineteenth century, were used by escaping slaves as codes. One song, "Wade in the Water," meant there was a river nearby and that using it as an escape route to the free states of the North was possible.

notebook during these times to write down his thoughts. Later in life, he would use notebooks as journals or to write notes for his choreography.

Early Inspiration

Even though they moved a lot, Alvin and his mother always knew where they would be on Sundays—at church. In Navasota, Lula's positive attitude was reinforced at the True Vine Baptist Church. During the service, the preacher would lead the congregation in spirituals. Spirituals are deeply emotional religious songs often with lyrics based on verses in the Bible.

Many of the pieces that Alvin later created were inspired by the spirituals that he heard as a boy. Two spirituals that inspired sections of *Revelations* (1960), his best-known dance, were "Take Me to the Water" and "I Want to Be Ready." He later called his memories of these spirituals and other childhood experiences "blood memories," memories and stories that were so deep inside him that they were part of his flesh and blood.

Alvin did not just find inspiration at church. Secular things would inspire some of his pieces, too, like the tough roadside bars that were all over the segregated southern United States at the time. The Dew Drop Inn in Navasota, Texas, inspired *Blues Suite* (1958). The

The Alvin Ailey American Dance Theater performs "I've Been 'Buked" from *Revelations*. In a tight, choirlike formation, the dancers look and reach upward for a sign of God. Ailey's dancers often felt that his themes helped them connect with the audience in ways that they never imagined.

Dew Drop Inn was a place some people went after a long, hard day at work. Even though Alvin was only about eight at the time, he would stand in the doorway and take in everything that was happening. Everything he saw and heard on these nights—the music, the dancing, the atmosphere of a party, the flashy clothing—would become the basis for *Blues Suite*, his first major work.

As much as Alvin loved living with Amos Alexander, Lula knew that Texas was not the best place for them. She thought there would be less racism—and more work—on the West Coast. This was during World War II, and most men were fighting overseas. There were many jobs for women on the West Coast in the defense industry. Before the war, men had held these jobs.

Alvin's mother went ahead to Los Angeles and found a good-paying job at an airplane factory. She was one of the first black women to work there. Alvin, twelve at the time, stayed on with Alexander until the end of the school term and then made the eighteen-hour train ride by himself.

2 Moving West

In Los Angeles, Alvin was enrolled in George Washington Carver Junior High School. He continued to write poetry and began a journal. He joined the glee club—a small-group chorus that sang a cappella, or without musical accompaniment. Alvin was large for his age. He could have been a football player, but he preferred gymnastics, handball, and track.

He excelled in school and always made the honor roll. Later, at Thomas Jefferson High School, Alvin was very good at foreign languages, especially French and Spanish. In fact, when Alvin's Spanish teacher was absent, Alvin would teach the class.

Alvin made his own meals and took care of the apartment when he came home from school and before his mother came home. When he was fourteen, his mother married a man named Fred Cooper. Alvin and his mother had been everything to each other for so many years, it took Alvin a while to adjust to the idea of having to share his mother with someone else. Soon, though, he realized that his mother was happy, and he came to love his new stepfather.

A Love of Dance Is Sparked

The first time Alvin had seen a dance performance was when he was in the seventh grade. His class went on a field trip to see a dance performance by the Ballet Russe de Monte Carlo at the Los Angeles Philharmonic Auditorium. The program included the Russian choreographer Vaslav Nijinsky's *L'Apres-Midi d'un Faun* (Afternoon of a Faun) and Mikhail

Fokine's *Schéhérazade*. Alvin's imagination was sparked by what he saw—concert dance, performed in a formal setting for an audience. He loved the dancers' movements and the costumes. He loved being in a theater.

Living in Los Angeles, Alvin had many opportunities to explore his growing love of dance. Alvin saw dance in the movies. He especially liked Fred Astaire and Gene Kelly, as well as the famed tap dance team the Nicholas Brothers. By the time he was fourteen, Alvin was spending most weekends in the theater district in Los Angeles, where he saw famous singers such as the legendary jazz and

Alvin Ailey

Mikhail Fokine and Vera Fokina in *Schéhérazade* in 1910. Fokine, a choreographer with the Ballet Russe, broke away from the traditional ballet style. In this piece, he was inspired by Arabian literature and costume.

blues singer Billie Holiday, the jazz musician and composer Duke Ellington, and the anthropologist and dancer Katherine Dunham, whose Tropical Revue showcased dance from the Caribbean.

Alvin first saw the Katherine Dunham Dance Company perform at the Biltmore Theater in Los Angeles in 1945. He said in his autobiography, *Revelations*, "I was taken into another realm. It was just a transcendent experience for me." Katherine Dunham had founded the first all-black ballet company in the United States in 1931. In 1945, she had just started the Dunham School of Dance and Theater in New York City. Little did Alvin know that he would work with her one day.

Although he was developing a love for dance, he didn't really put it together

16

yet that he wanted to dance. He was, however, beginning to get the idea that dance was an athletic sport and that the dance movements he saw were similar to what he loved about gymnastics.

Entering the World of Dance

One day, his friend Carmen de Lavallade, whom he was quite fond of, danced in a school assembly. Alvin thought she was terrific. Alvin was focusing on gymnastics at the time, but when Carmen said to Alvin, "You ought to be a dancer," he decided to give it a try.

Carmen was taking dance classes at the Lester Horton Dance Theater.

Katherine Dunham is pictured here in *L'Ag'Ya*, a piece inspired by a fighting dance known as ag'ya, which she had seen in the Caribbean. She brought the experience of African cultural roots to American concert dance.

Lester Horton was a modern dance choreographer. He made very theatrical dances often based on themes of social injustice. He founded his own dance company in 1932 and later opened a school and theater in Hollywood in 1946. His students learned many forms of dance, and they learned how to cooperate artistically to create new dances. They also learned how to make sets and costumes.

Because Alvin liked Carmen, he went along with her to Horton's school. What Alvin saw there was just about the most exciting thing he had ever seen. He saw black dancers and white dancers taking class together, which was really unusual in 1948. He saw dancers practicing exciting movements that used the torso in new and different ways. He saw costumes of all colors, drums along one wall, mobiles hanging from the ceiling, and walls painted different colors.

The Birth of Modern Dance

Modern dance is a form of dance that developed in the early part of the twentieth century in Europe and America. Artists rebelling against the stylistic conventions of classical ballet created the first modern dances. These choreographers wanted to create dances that were capable of expressing the kinds of feelings, thoughts, and images they were experiencing in the new century.

Carmen de Lavallade is pictured here in 1955. She had won a scholarship to study with Lester Horton at age sixteen, then became his lead dancer.

Lester Horton, like other modern dance choreographers, was interested in all the different ways the body can move. Horton's style of dancing and the technique he taught focused on moving through space while stretching the body in an almost infinite range of motion. It required tremendous strength from the dancers.

At first, Alvin was too shy to join in, and for weeks, he simply watched Carmen take classes. Soon, though, he realized that if he was good at gymnastics, he might be strong enough to try one of Horton's classes. As soon as he gave it a try, he knew he had made the right decision. He loved it. Horton thought that Alvin had talent and encouraged him to consider dance as a career.

A Tug in Two Directions

After he graduated from high school in 1948, Alvin

went to the University of California at Los Angeles (UCLA) to study foreign languages. He was planning to become a teacher. At the same time, he was drawn back to Lester Horton and his challenging technique, democratic working style, and racially integrated company.

The next year, in 1949, he transferred to San Francisco State College to live away from home for a while. He worked long hours to pay his tuition. Sometimes, he had only about four hours at home to sleep, eat, and do his homework. More and more, Alvin found himself thinking back to the warmth and camaraderie of the Lester Horton group. He transferred to Los Angeles City College and dove into dance at the same time.

Alvin was now about twenty-two. He proved to be a strong and magnetic dancer even though he had gotten a late start. Most dancers begin to study for a professional career at around age ten or even earlier. Now, as if to make up for lost time, Alvin took as many classes as he could. He also taught the children's classes. That same year, Lester Horton invited Alvin to join the company.

His powerful presence on stage began to attract attention. He and Carmen were invited by the jazz choreographer Jack Cole to dance in a Hollywood film, *Lydia Bailey*. He loved working with Jack Cole, and he loved dancing with Carmen. Alvin was beginning to get the idea that this might be his life's work. He was happy that he was dancing in Lester Horton's company, but things were about to change in unexpected ways.

The year was 1953. Unexpectedly and tragically, Lester Horton suffered a heart attack and died. At the time, the company was preparing for a performance at Jacob's Pillow, a summer dance school and festival in the Berkshire Mountains in Massachusetts founded by modern dance pioneer Ted Shawn. The company had

a commitment and had no director and no dances to perform.

Frank Eng, the company's general manager, invited all the company members to submit their own work to be considered for the performance. Because Alvin had always made notes for his own choreography in his journals, he had ideas ready. He submitted three ideas: a solo for company member James Truitte, which would be a tribute to Horton called *According to Saint Francis*; a piece for Carmen, called *Mourning, Morning*, inspired by the work of playwright Tennessee Williams; and a dance based on the story of Adam and Eve called

Alvin Ailey is pictured here at an early stage in his career. There were not many opportunities for black dancers in the 1940s and 1950s. Little did Ailey know at this time that he was about to embark on a career that would bring black culture into the mainstream of dance.

Creation of the World. No one else had come up with anything, so Alvin was appointed the company choreographer.

Alvin had never actually choreographed anything before, but he had watched Lester Horton at work. Unlike many types of art, which are created in isolation, dance is a collaboration between the choreographer and the dancers. While the choreographer may have an idea ahead of time, he or she works movements out with the dancers directly in the rehearsal process. This was especially true of Lester Horton, who often gave his dancers individual movement assignments to work out during rehearsals and welcomed their creative contributions.

Even though Alvin had participated in this process with Horton, the first pieces he choreographed were much too long and received negative reviews when they were performed at Jacob's Pillow. As Alvin wrote in his autobiography about *Mourning, Morning*, "It was so confusing, I am sure that nobody knew what was going on onstage."

Alvin had gotten his feet wet in the world of professional dance, and he was eager to learn more. Yet he didn't necessarily want to stay on as choreographer for Lester Horton's company. An opportunity presented itself immediately. In December 1954, Alvin and Carmen were offered jobs dancing in the Broadway musical *House of Flowers*, starring Pearl Bailey and written by novelist Truman Capote with music by Harold Arlen and choreography by Herb Ross.

They were to work in Philadelphia, where at that time many shows bound for Broadway were rehearsed and first performed. Alvin told his mother that he was heading east and would be back in six months. Little did he know that New York would be his home base for the rest of his life.

3 From Los Angeles to New York

In the 1950s, New York City was the center of the performing arts in the United States. After the successful run of *House of Flowers*, Ailey appeared in the movie *Carmen Jones* (1954) and the Broadway musical *Sing Man Sing* (1956) starring Harry Belafonte. He studied with all the great masters of modern dance who were teaching in New York at the time. Among them were modern dance pioneers Charles Weidman and Doris Humphrey. From them, he learned to explore movement as a constant process of falling off balance and recovering to find balance once again. Ailey took classes from Martha Graham, another of the great pioneers of modern dance. He learned her technique of initiating movement by contracting and releasing the muscles at the core, or center, of the body. Ailey also studied with Katherine Dunham, whose low-to-the-ground movements evoked the dances of the West Indies.

He studied at the New Dance Group with the next generation of modern dance choreographers, including Anna Sokolow. He also studied ballet and jazz. Ailey knew that all these different styles would help him have more control and flexibility when he performed and when he created his own pieces.

Ailey soaked up the entire New York arts scene. An old friend from San Francisco State College, Marguerite Angelos, had also moved to New York where she was writing poetry under the name Maya Angelou. He also met other important African American writers, including Langston Hughes. Ailey began to think about his goals. He wanted to form a dance company that took elements from the theater— the dramatic lighting, the staging, and the colorful costumes—and combine them with the dynamic movements of dance. He wanted to talk about the African American experience from a very personal point of view. He wanted to feature mostly African American dancers and choreographers.

Blues Suite

In 1957, Ailey was performing in another Broadway show, *Jamaica*, starring Lena Horne and Ricardo Montalban and choreographed by Jack Cole. He performed on Broadway at night and

Poet, activist, and author Maya Angelou is pictured on her one and only singing album, *Miss Calypso*, in 1957. She was twenty-seven years old.

rented a studio where he could work on his own choreography during the day. He and another dancer, Ernest Parham, began to plan an evening-long program to be held at the Young Men's/ Young Women's Hebrew Association on Ninety-second Street in New York City (known as the 92nd Street Y). Dancers from *Jamaica* and other plays on Broadway were to present various pieces. Ailey choreographed a solo for himself, called *Ode and Homage*, which honored Lester Horton, and a new group dance to end the evening.

Ailey invited six dancers to help him create the new piece. Some were from Lester Horton's company, and a few were dancers he had met in New York. They worked with Ailey at night after their regular jobs or in the late afternoons when Ailey and others were performing on Broadway in the evenings.

Ailey wanted to re-create through dance the sights and sounds of the Dew Drop Inn and other bars he had seen when he was growing up in Texas. He wanted audiences to know where the blues came from. As he wrote in the program notes, "From the fields and barrelhouses of the Southern Negro sprang the blues—songs of lost love, despair, protest, and anger—hymns to the secular region of his soul."

To achieve this, the new dance was to have ten short sections, each one named after a blues song that Ailey had heard when he was a child, such as "Good Morning, Blues," "House of the Rising Sun," and "Mean Ol' Frisco." He had an image in his head of what he wanted each short piece to look like. Some would show men and women dancing and having a good time. Some would show people fighting. He would show anger and sadness as well as joy and humor.

Ailey demonstrated the movements he wanted from each of his dancers. He described to his dancers what each character in the piece was like. The dancers worked hard to help make his vision real. The rehearsals were demanding and exhausting, but the dancers didn't mind. According to

Sounds of Ailey's Childhood

Everything that went into *Blues Suite* came from Ailey's childhood. Years later, in his autobiography *Revelations*, his mother recalled the inspiration for the train whistle in *Blues Suite*. "Alvin got that when we lived in Rogers . . . we didn't live too far from the railroad tracks."

dance historian Elizabeth Zimmer, one dancer he worked with said, "He had the knack of making you tear your guts out on stage. You really wanted to give it all you had." They knew they were working with a choreographer destined for greatness, someone who would make his mark in the world of modern dance.

On March 30, 1958, the new dance called *Blues Suite* had its premiere at the Kaufmann Auditorium at the 92nd Street Y, and it was an immediate hit. *New York Times* critic John Martin called the whole evening "an impressive debut," praising especially *Blues Suite*, which he said was "overflowing with variety, beautifully staged with excellent décor . . . and on this occasion was superbly danced." Alvin Ailey, he said, had "a rich animal quality of movement and an innate sense of theatrical projection."

Hard Work and Long Hours

Ailey and the other dancers had spent a long time preparing for that one evening's performance. Even though the performance was a critical success, it didn't translate into immediate fame and fortune. No producer rushed up to them after the show with a contract in hand for a world tour. Ailey's dancers went back to their jobs during the day and their rigorous rehearsal schedules at night.

Ailey found places for his group to perform in the New York area. They drove to each performance in an old station wagon. They performed in costumes they made themselves. Ailey's apartment at this time was jammed with costumes and props. Often, Ailey couldn't afford to pay his dancers at all, and when he did, it was usually no more than $15 per performance.

In 1959, Ailey started work in the studio on another piece. This time, he decided to reach back into his blood memories and talk about going to church in Texas with his mother. The result was *Revelations*, a suite of dances revealing the scope of African American religious experience to the accompaniment of a variety of spiritual and gospel pieces. The opening section to "I've Been 'Buked" is a carefully sculpted abstract image of a fervent group prayer. The central section, called "Take Me to the Water," is inspired by a baptism Ailey had seen when he was a child. A group of dancers, dressed in white, forms a procession across the stage. Long strips of blue silk are then spread across the stage to represent water, and a baptism is performed to the spiritual "Wade in the Water." A fast-paced athletic section, "Sinner Man," features three men tormented by their sins. The final section of the piece, "Move, Members, Move," begins with women of the church sitting on stools and fanning themselves in the hot Texas sun. Indeed, his mother and other women of the church were the

inspiration for this scene. The section ends in a rousing celebration in which the whole company dances to "Rocka My Soul in the Bosom of Abraham."

Revelations premiered on January 31, 1960, at the Kaufmann Auditorium at the 92nd Street Y. The standing ovation at this first performance was long and thunderous. Critics the next day declared *Revelations* a masterpiece. *New York Times* critic John Martin called it "an infinitely moving hymn to God, and perhaps more, man."

Later that year, in October 1960, Ailey's group was invited to become the resident company at the Clark Center for the Performing Arts, at

Three Ailey dancers perform "Wade in the Water" from *Revelations* in 1977. The woman holding the umbrella symbolizes a deaconess, ceremoniously leading new converts to the riverbank for the baptism. The river, symbolized by two strips of blue silk, is in the background.

the YWCA on Eighth Avenue and Fifty-first Street in New York City. Being a resident company meant that they had a home base in New York with studio space for their rehearsals.

An Outstanding Decade of Career Triumphs

When John F. Kennedy was president, First Lady Jacqueline Kennedy saw the company perform and urged her husband to consider this dynamic African American group of dancers for the role of cultural ambassadors. So, in 1962, the Alvin Ailey American Dance Theater was selected by the State Department to perform abroad as part of the president's International Exchange Program. They embarked on a tour of Southeast Asia and Australia. On the tour, the world stood up and cheered.

The company made its first major U.S. tour in 1968. They performed in large theaters to sold-out audiences. By then, Ailey had stopped dancing and was choreographing full-time in addition to running his ever-growing dance company. He was ready to take the next step in realizing his goals. He wanted his company to have a permanent home and a school.

In 1969, he achieved both goals at once. He founded the Alvin Ailey American Dance Center (now called The Ailey School) in Brooklyn, one of the boroughs of New York City, as a home for both his company and school. As the school grew over the years, it would move to larger quarters. First the school moved to a converted church on Fifty-ninth Street in New York City, and then to a building in Times Square in the theater district. Next it moved to West Sixty-first Street, near Lincoln Center for the

Performing Arts. While the company rehearsed in the school's studios, it performed in many different theaters during its New York season over the years. Finally, in 1972 the company became the resident dance company of the City Center Theater on West Fifty-fifth Street, where they still perform each December through New Year's.

Also in this period of Ailey's career, he was invited to create dances for many other important companies and events that stretched him in new creative directions. In 1962, he choreographed *Feast of Ashes* for the Joffrey Ballet. This dance, based on *The*

House of Bernarda Alba by Spanish writer Federico Garcia Lorca, is considered by many dance critics to be the first successful ballet on pointe created by a modern dance choreographer. In 1966, he created the dances for *Antony and Cleopatra* composed by Samuel Barber. This important production was the New York City Metropolitan Opera's inaugural performance at Lincoln Center for the Performing Arts. In 1970, he combined jazz movement with ballet technique to create *The River*, a new ballet with a score by the great jazz composer Duke Ellington for the American Ballet Theater. In 1971, Ailey staged composer

Pictured here are the ill-fated lovers Adela and Pepe in *Feast of Ashes*, the first classical ballet choreographed by Ailey. Ailey was drawn to ballet for its technical range and the line that it gives a dancer's body. Yet he wanted to give an audience the experience of emotions he felt only modern dance could capture.

Leonard Bernstein's rock-influenced *Mass* as the opening production of the John F. Kennedy Center for the Performing Arts, a national showplace for the arts in Washington, D.C.

Meanwhile, he was still creating works for his own company. *Masekela Langage*, first performed in 1969, was inspired by political events of the time. The setting was similar to that of *Blues Suite*. It is a bar, but this bar is in Johannesburg, South Africa. It takes place during the time of apartheid, or the racial segregation that existed in South Africa from 1948 into the 1990s. The music is that of trumpeter Hugh Masekela, who was an antiapartheid activist.

Cry, choreographed in 1971, was a gift to Ailey's mother for her birthday. He dedicated the piece to "all Black women everywhere—especially our mothers." This sixteen-minute solo danced by Judith Jamison celebrates the struggles and triumphs of the black woman in America. The three sections of the dance are set to music by Alice Coltrane, Laura Nyro, and the Voices of East Harlem. The piece received rave reviews. Clive Barnes of the *New York Times* called it "a sensation. Rarely have a choreographer and dancer been in such accord."

A Rich Life Cut Short

On December 1, 1989, at age 58, Alvin Ailey died of a blood disorder. The world of dance gathered to mourn him. The Cathedral of Saint John the Divine in New York City was filled to capacity with 4,000 mourners at his memorial service. Dancers performed sections from *Cry* and from *Revelations*. The audience, including his

Bidding farewell to the great choreographer, members of Ailey's company are pictured here during "I've Been 'Buked" from *Revelations* at Ailey's funeral service on December 8, 1989. This signature work was fitting as a tribute. It evokes feelings of a common sacred experience shared among a large, diverse group of people.

mother, cried with love and pride at the son they were sending home. In a poem she read at the service, Maya Angelou said about Alvin Ailey, "When great trees fall, rocks on distant hills shudder."

From New York to the World: Alvin Ailey's Legacy

When I think of Alvin Ailey," Judith Jamison wrote in her autobiography, *Dancing Spirit*, "I think of rivers, the clarity and strength of water, carrying with it the memory of its source as it pushes forward. I think of winding rivers, of water brimming with life."

Alvin Ailey's life had begun near the Brazos River in Texas and through its winding course had gathered strength and reached its end in New York City. He often said, "I believe dance came from the people and it should always be delivered back to the people." He did just that in his lifetime. When he died, he was known the world over.

During his life, Alvin Ailey received all the highest honors in the worlds of dance and culture, from the Gold Star at the 1970 International Dance Festival in Paris, France, to the prestigious Spingarn Medal in 1976, awarded annually by the NAACP for "outstanding achievement by a black American." In 1988, he received a John F. Kennedy Center Honor for Lifetime Achievement in the Performing Arts.

Alvin Ailey presented work that was unique to the world of dance in his time. He blended elements from many different styles, from African dance to ballet and from social dances to modern dance, to create his uniquely theatrical and emotion-packed dances. Audiences had never seen anything like *Revelations*, *Blues Suite*, or *Cry*. His dances revealed a world that was not well-known to the people who usually attended ballet and modern dance performances at that time. He made dances about things that were very real and specific to African American people, but to which everyone could relate. And he filled auditoriums and theaters all over the world!

Still Going Strong

The Alvin Ailey American Dance Theater is still going strong today and shows no sign of letting up. The company has performed for five American presidents, on six continents, and at three summer Olympics. There is a U.S. postage stamp featuring Alvin Ailey and a street in New York City called Alvin Ailey Place, West Sixty-first Street, between Amsterdam Avenue and West End Avenue.

Anna Kisselgoff of the *New York Times* has written that the group's "phenomenal popularity is unmatched by any other company in the world." And Mayor Michael Bloomberg of New York City declared December 23, 2003, Alvin Ailey American Dance Theater Day. It was the forty-fifth anniversary of the first performance of Ailey's choreography at the 92nd Street Y.

Ailey wanted to preserve great works in modern dance and showcase them in his company. By 1974, he had revived many classic modern dance pieces. Above, men of the Ailey company perform Ted Shawn's *Kinetic Molpai*. Shawn choreographed numerous innovative, vigorous pieces for male dancers.

Alvin Ailey created seventy-nine ballets in his lifetime. Many of his pieces are still performed by his company. Some have been performed by other companies throughout the world, including the Paris Opera Ballet, London Festival Ballet, and the Royal Danish Ballet. Many of his pieces have been videotaped for the archives of the New York Public Library of Performing Arts at Lincoln Center.

Over the years, more than seventy choreographers have had their work performed by the Alvin Ailey American Dance Theater. Some of these choreographers have included Dr. Pearl Primus, Talley Beatty, Donald McKayle, Ulysses Dove, Garth Fagan, Judith Jamison, George Faison, and Ronald K. Brown.

Alvin Ailey's dream of a dance company that primarily presents the work of African American dancers

An Ailey Alum's "Rich" Tip

One of the Ailey dancers, Dudley Williams, tells new company members that if they put aside one dollar every time they performed "Rev" (as *Revelations* is known to the dancers), they'll be rich! Williams has had a rich career. He celebrated his fortieth anniversary with the company in 2004.

Dudley Williams began dancing at age twelve. He won a scholarship to the Juilliard School and danced with various companies, including the Martha Graham Company, which he left in 1964 to become a member of Ailey's company. In 1972, Ailey was inspired to create a dance especially for Williams's talents called *Love Songs*.

and choreographers is carried on every day by Judith Jamison, who has been the company's artistic director since Ailey died in 1989. "He has left me a road map. It's very clear. It works," she wrote in her autobiography.

In 2004, the company and school moved to a permanent home, built just for them. The Alvin Ailey American Dance Theater and The Ailey School are

Judith Jamison, pictured here in 1979, was discovered in Philadelphia by Agnes de Mille in 1964. She joined Ailey's company the next year. She became the company's artistic director at his request.

now located at Fifty-fifth Street and Ninth Avenue in New York City.

Today, the school has many programs for all levels, from three-year-olds beginning the First Steps program in the junior division to college students earning the Ailey School/Fordham University bachelor of fine arts (BFA) degree, a four-year college program that offers dance training and a liberal arts education. Many of the dancers with the Alvin Ailey American Dance Theater began by studying at the school.

Former company members teach at The Ailey School and at AileyCamp, dance camps around the country started by Ailey in Kansas City in 1989. Ailey's legacy is passed on from one generation to the next every day, from those who knew him and danced with him to those who are learning his signature work, *Revelations*, for the first time.

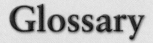

Glossary

accessible Easy to understand and appreciate, without need for any special knowledge.

anthropologist A person who studies the customs of different cultures.

blues Music that developed from African American folk songs.

choreographer Someone who creates and arranges dance movement.

jazz Music developed by African Americans in New Orleans in the late nineteenth century.

on pointe In ballet technique, balancing or dancing on the extreme tips of the toes in specially designed shoes.

premiere The first public performance of a dance piece, movie, or play.

program notes Background information gathered in a booklet given to audience members at a dance or theater performance.

repertory The group of dances that a dance company performs.

secular Not religious.

segregation Keeping people separated, usually by race.

technique In dance, a specific way of using the body, time, space, and dynamics to create a movement style.

For More Information

Alvin Ailey American Dance Theater
The Joan Weill Center for Dance
405 West 55th Street
New York, NY 10019-4402
(212) 405-9000
Web site: http://www.alvinailey.org

Dance Magazine and *Young Dancer*
333 Seventh Avenue, 11th Floor
New York, NY 10001
(212) 979-4803
e-mail: dancemag@dancemagazine.com
Web site: http://www.dancemagazine.com

The Katherine Dunham Centers for Arts
and Humanities
532 North 10th Street
East St. Louis, IL 62201
(618) 271-3367
e-mail: dunham@primary.net
Web site: http://www.eslarp.uiuc.edu/kdunham

Web Sites

Due to the changing nature of Internet links, the
Rosen Publishing Group, Inc., has developed an
on-line list of Web sites related to the subject of this
book. This site is updated regularly. Please use
this link to access the list:

http://www.rosenlinks.com/lac/alai

For Further Reading

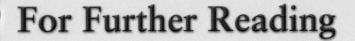

Ailey, Alvin, and A. Peter Bailey. *Revelations: The Autobiography of Alvin Ailey.* New York, NY: Birch Lane Press, Carol Publishing Group, 1995.

Hamilton, Linda H., Ph.D. *Advice for Dancers: Emotional Counsel and Practical Strategies.* San Francisco, CA: Jossey-Bass Publishers, 1998.

Lewis-Ferguson, Julinda. *Alvin Ailey, Jr.: A Life in Dance.* New York, NY: Walker Publishing Company, Inc., 1994.

Solomon Probosz, Kathilyn. *Alvin Ailey, Jr.* New York, NY: Bantam Skylark, 1992.

Bibliography

Ailey, Alvin, and A. Peter Bailey. *Revelations: The Autobiography of Alvin Ailey.* New York, NY: Birch Lane Press, Carol Publishing Group, 1995.

DeFrantz, Thomas F. *Dancing Revelations: Alvin Ailey's Embodiment of African-American Culture.* New York, NY: Oxford University Press, 2004.

Dunning, Jennifer. *Alvin Ailey: A Life in Dance.* New York, NY: Addison-Wesley Publishing Company, Inc., 1996.

Jamison, Judith. *Dancing Spirit: An Autobiography with Howard Kaplan.* New York, NY: Doubleday, 1993.

Index

About the Author

Judy Gitenstein is an editor and writer who lives in New York City. She edited a previous biography of Alvin Ailey for young readers (*Alvin Ailey, Jr.* by Kathilyn Solomon Probosz) and currently edits The Ailey® School Newsletter.

Photo Credits

Cover © Deborah Feingold/Getty Images; cover (background), pp. 1, 32 © Sahm Doherty/Time Life Pictures/Getty Images; pp. 5, 12, 35, 40 © Jerome Robbins Dance Division, the New York Public Library for the Performing Arts, Astor, Lenox and Tilden Foundations; p. 9 courtesy of Judy Gitenstein; p. 16 © Hulton Archive/Getty Images; p. 17 © Bettmann/Corbis; p. 19 © Library of Congress, Prints and Photographs Division, Carl Van Vechten Collection (LC-USZ62-114408); p. 22 © Library of Congress, Prints and Photographs Division; p. 27 © Gene Lester/Getty Images; pp. 37, 43 © AP/Wide World Photos; p. 42 © Jack Mitchell.

Design: Tahara Anderson
Editor: Leigh Ann Cobb
Developmental Editor: Nancy Allison, CMA, RME